For this

Child

I

Prayed

For this

Child

I

Prayed

A Practical Guide to Biblical Parenting

Linda P. Jones

Published by Linda P. Jones

Printed by CreateSpace Publishing
CreateSpace, a DBA of on-Demand Publishing, LLC

ISBN-10: 1508929157
ISBN-13: 978-1508929154

CONTENTS

FOREWORD

In today's world, when we acquire a new car, a new appliance, a computer, and even a phone, they each come with a manual. There we can learn how best to handle the new treasure, how to provide adequate care, and very importantly, there is often a warning list of "what not to do." Some bemoan the fact that children do not arrive with a manual. Actually a manual does exist, but it is couched within the larger more comprehensive volume: the manual for life. Yes there is such a manual, and it is known to us as the Bible; God's words of wisdom and revelation to mankind. However, the wisdom and knowledge we need is interspersed with historical records, tucked away in proverbs, and mixed in with many other themes of life; so unearthing the ones specifically about raising children, for the uninitiated, can be like digging for buried treasure without a clear map. In this book, Linda Jones has done much of the digging for us, and provided pointers so we can continue in time to discover more treasures for ourselves.

Not only has Linda provided some choice nuggets of truth, but she has shared from practical experience including her own. Whether or not this is your first child, it is always comforting to know that the challenges of parenthood are universal, and that there is no super- parent who has it all together. Nevertheless, tried and true advice is available for us as parents seeking to do the very best for our children. In this book, you will find the charming mix of human experience and Godly wisdom to help walk with you through the maze of how to raise this child to be a well-balanced human being, a good citizen who respects his/herself as well as respecting the rights of others, one who seeks to do what its right, loves kindness, and desires to walk humbly with God (Micah 6:8). This is a tall order, but it is still God's commission to us as parents, and this small book contains many choice treasures of advice which will help you along the journey.

For this reason, "The Rock" Christian School has made this the book of choice as a welcome gift for new parents.

Please, take time to read this book cover to cover. It is an investment of time you will not regret. Our children are too precious to only rely on trial and error, so we must learn from those who have successfully gone before us, and from the words of our Lord, as we sit at his feet like the disciples of old. Enjoy and be blessed.

Marcia Jenkins (Mrs.)
Administrator
"The Rock" Christian School Inc.

PREFACE

This book is written primarily with a new generation of parents in mind, some of whom were not competently parented themselves, and therefore, have no positive role models to follow, but are now expected to be good parents to their children. There is formal training for just about every profession, but there is very little in the way of training parents for the most important task in the universe, rearing children.

For this Child I Prayed is designed to encourage parents in their endeavours as co-labourers with God to raise righteous seed for God's kingdom; a generation that would show forth His glory in the earth. It is by no means a comprehensive book on parenting, but it is easy reading, with tips, guides, poems and prayers; something a parent can refer to again and again. Whether you are the biological parent of a child or have the responsibility of raising children either through adoption, fostering, step parenting or grand parenting, this book will be of help to you.

ACKNOWLEDGEMENTS

Special thanks to the many friends who loaned their support and writing skills to help in the first editing of the work.

Special appreciation to my husband for his encouragement and belief in me to be able to complete this mandate.

Thank you Holy Spirit, for impregnating me with this God-idea and for the spiritual insights and truths you kept on revealing especially at times when I felt I hadn't much more to write.

INTRODUCTION

In the opening chapters of the Old Testament Book of 1Samuel, we have the story of Hannah, the wife of Elkanah. Hannah was barren and she petitioned the Lord for a male child whom she promised to return to the Lord after he was weaned. God graciously answered her prayer, and she gave birth to a son whom she named Samuel. After Hannah had weaned the child she then fulfilled her vow to the Lord to *give him to the Lord all the days of his life* (1Samuel 1:11).

Verses 24-28 tell us how she took Samuel and presented him to Eli the high priest, and as she presented him, she stated resolutely:

> *"For this child I prayed and the Lord has granted me my petition which I asked of Him. Therefore I also have lent him to the Lord; as long as he lives he shall be lent to the Lord."*

> — *1Samuel 1:27-28*

The Scripture said Hannah lent Samuel to the Lord. The word *lent* does not have quite the same meaning in this sentence as we understand in English. Hannah was the one who was *lent* the child. The Hebrew expresses the meaning of *lent* here as meaning that she asked for Samuel as a loan from the Lord, she obtained him by petitioning, but then she returned him to the Lord for

His use or employment. The Scripture also stated that Samuel was first weaned, and then she took him to appear before the Lord. The word "weaned" comes from the Hebrew *gamal*, which means "to treat a person well, to benefit, or to ripen." Hannah understood, that as a parent she had the responsibility of preparing, or *ripening her* child before presenting him to the Lord for His use.

For This Child I Prayed is one of the many tools available to help parents in the process as they *gamal*, i.e., ripen, or treat well their children. It is designed to assist parents in doing every positive thing to benefit their children, as they work with the Holy Spirit in detaching them from the natural tendency of the sin nature, which is in rebellion against God, and in redirecting them into a place where they can stand before God and experience Him for themselves.

I pray that the Holy Spirit, the One Who directs into all truth, the Helper, will give us parents, all we need to raise up a godly seed for the Father.

Note

When we hear the word *child* our minds almost immediately think of a young child somewhere between infancy and five or six years of age. In the Scriptures, however, and in this book, the term is used in a broader sense referring to the period from infancy to a young man even as Chuck Swindoll suggests, "to a marriageable age." As long as that child is under the care of the parent, that parent is responsible for his or her training.

CHAPTER 1
THE VALUE OF A CHILD

Treat your children as though you won't have them next year. Train your children as though they won't have you next year.

— *Sandy Simmons*

Your Child is a Gift from God

"Behold, children are a heritage from the Lord"

(Psalm 127:3a)

The Hebrew word for heritage carries the meaning of a possession granted by Jehovah, a gift of Jehovah. The child God has given you, is His very property, His gift! Think about it, He has deemed you trustworthy to be given the "power of attorney" in this child's life. What an awesome privilege to be entrusted with God's possession. You must then ask yourself how you are caring for and handling this precious gift from God. Am I modelling Christ-like attitudes and behaviour in the home? Am I using every opportunity to train in godly principles and values? Do I respect and appreciate this gift of God?

Too many children today are left to figure out what is right or wrong for themselves. They learn from and imitate their peers who themselves are often misguided, or they learn from the media which many times have no commitment to godly values. As you understand the intrinsic value in the wonderful gift God has given you through this child, you are challenged to do everything within your power to see that your child is well cared for, and personally introduced to his God and Creator.

Your Child is a Reward from God

"The fruit of the womb is His reward"

(Psalm 127:3b)

To reward means to give something in return, and in a true sense, children are God's token of favour; they are His prize to a man and woman for their love, commitment and trust to each other. God's plan is that children are to be reared in a home where they are parented by a father and mother who are married. Unfortunately in our sin-stained world, man has fallen short of that standard. Children are conceived and born out of wedlock, through incest, as a result of rape or from adulterous relationships. In spite of all these, children are still God's reward to man. Incidentally, there are no illegitimate children, just parents who have acted illegitimately by violating God's law.

Your Child is an Arrow

"Like arrows in the hand of a warrior, so are the children of one's youth. Happy is the man who has his quiver full of them..."

(Psalm 127:4,5a)

There are several things to learn from the imagery of the arrow in regard to our children. Arrows are instruments intended for action, they strike from afar and suddenly; they are long-range, lightning-quick and unseen. Arrows are also prime symbols of divine justice. What powerful symbols that speak of the value of children. As instruments of action and power, arrows are missiles intended for specific targets. God has destined our children for particular targets. They are weapons of offence which God puts in the hands of parents who ought to be mighty, warriors and powerful in prayer. Parents who have known battle and victory can now train their young arrows to be the same.

The quiver is where arrows are kept for safekeeping until the time when they are ready to be released. God has committed into the quiver of every parent, specially designed arrows. But just as it takes skill and practice to master the art of archery, it takes expertise and wisdom to master the art of child rearing. Parents must therefore take on the challenge of keeping their arrows sharp and ready, and apply all their parenting skills to successfully direct and launch them into life, into the world, and to meet the enemy face to face and not be disgraced or confounded.

Your Child was Formed and Known by God in the Womb

"Before I formed you in the womb I knew you..."

(Jeremiah 1:5)

"For you have formed my inward parts; You covered me in my mother's womb, I will praise you, for I am fearfully and wonderfully made; marvellous are Your works and that my soul knows very well. My frame was not hidden from You, when I was made in secret, and skilfully wrought in the lowest parts of the earth. Your eyes saw substance, being yet unformed"

(Psalm 139:13-16)

This child was in God's heart even before being intricately formed in the womb. This child is really God's idea, not yours. The circumstances of conception may not have been His plan or yours, but each child is God's original idea.

Your Child has a God-Ordained Plan for His Life

"Before you were born I sanctified you and ordained you a prophet to the nation"

(Jeremiah 1:5).

Jocebed, Moses' mother saw that he was a beautiful child, and hid him rather than allow him to be thrown into the river. To the ancients, beauty was a sign of divine approval, and to Jocebed it meant that God had some special design concerning Moses. She saw the mark of divine favour on her son and purposed not to let it die. Through God's intervention, Pharaoh's daughter discovered Moses by the riverbank and in time His plan for him was fulfilled; Moses became the instrument He used to deliver the children of Israel from Egyptian bondage.

Hannah and Elkanah parented Samuel with purpose; they did everything that was in their ability to prepare him for the calling of God on his life. She fulfilled her vow to the Lord by giving him back to the Lord and Samuel became the first judge and national prophet of Israel.

Your child has a specific calling of God on his or her life, placed there before the foundation of the world. This child has a destiny which only he or she can fulfil. There is a unique aspect of God's glory that this child is meant to reveal to the world, and the world is awaiting it. With that in mind, parenting is to be done with purpose and confidence.

Your Child is Like an Olive Plant

"...Your children like olive plants all around your table."

(Psalm 128:3b)

The olive tree is an evergreen tree with a long life and great productive force. It symbolizes vitality, stability and continuance. The oil expressed from the fruit is high in nutritional value and used for making other very useful products. As olive plants, our children are rich in resources; properly cared for and tilled, they will be strong, productive and enduring, able to withstand the tests and storms of life.

This gift, this reward, this arrow and olive plant, formed in the womb of the mother is filled with the pre-ordained purpose of God. This child is in your hand to love, train and mould to become a blessing for God's glory. What an honour God bestows upon a parent.

A Parent's Prayer

Lord, I need your help today.
I want to care for those you've sent into my life,
to help them grow in body, mind and spirit,
to help them develop the special gifts
You've given them.
But I also want to free them
to follow their own paths
and bring their loving wisdom
to the world.
Help me to embrace them without clutching,
To support them without suffocating
To correct them without crushing.
And help me to live joyfully and playfully
myself so they can see Your life in me
and find their way to You.

Amen.

—Anonymous

CHAPTER 2
IMPARTING YOUR FAITH TO YOUR CHILDREN

Kids today learn a lot about getting to the moon, but very little about getting to heaven.

— *David Jeremiah*

In the Jewish culture, the religious education of children was the parent's responsibility. Their major concern was that their children come to know the living God. They took seriously the Lord's instruction in Deuteronomy 6:4-9, also known as the Shema, to teach their children diligently the commands of the Lord.

"Hear, O Israel: The Lord our God, the Lord is one! You shall love the Lord your God with all your heart, with all your soul, and with all your strength. And these words which I command you today shall be in your heart; you shall teach them diligently to your children and shall talk of them when you sit in your house, when you walk by the way, when you lie down, and when you rise up. You shall bind them as a sign on your hand and they shall be as frontlets

between your eyes. You shall write them on the doorposts of your house and on your gates."

This Scripture is the biblical mandate that God has given to parents for the training of their children. Therefore it is not the prime responsibility of the Sunday School Teacher or the school system to give your child a moral and biblical education.

Mary and Joseph obviously followed the directives of the Word of God because by the time Jesus was age twelve, He knew the Old Testament Scriptures well enough that He was able to converse with the rabbis in the temple, asking questions and astounding them with His wisdom and understanding of the Law (Luke 2:41-50).

The Apostle Paul encouraged Timothy to continue in what he had been taught from the Scriptures during his childhood, which were the Old Testament writings (2Timothy 3:14,15). This word **childhood** literally means "from a babe." Timothy's mother and grandmother started instructing him in the Scriptures from very early infancy (see 1:5). This is not something that is difficult for parents to do today, considering all the teaching tools that are available, such as bible storybooks, videos, DVD's, games and toys. The parents of Old Testament times were not so privileged as we are today, yet they got the job done.

The Apostle also said that it is the Scriptures that will give guidance into the experience of salvation. The parent who diligently plants the seed of the Word of God on the soil of the heart of their children is more likely to reap the harvest of them coming to the knowledge of salvation at a very early age. The responsibility of the parent according to the Scripture is to write the law on the heart of the child; it is the child in co-operation with the Holy Spirit that puts it in his heart. *"The word have I hid in my heart that I might not sin against Thee"* (Psalm 119:11).

Five Ways to Impart your Faith to your Children

1. By Principle. There were very few formal schools in the Old Testament time. Most learning took place in the context of everyday life and as opportunities arose throughout the day, parents would instruct their children. Jesus used this teaching method as He taught His disciples. He used everyday occurrences that were familiar to the disciples to impart teachings they would not forget. For example, the scene of the farmer sowing seeds would be commonplace as they travelled the land of Palestine, and Jesus used this picture to teach the message of the Kingdom.

The Scripture in Deuteronomy involves what can be called the formal and informal method of teaching. *"You shall talk of them when you sit in your house"* (vs. 7a). This I consider the formal approach. There are to be specific times set apart for bible reading, stories, discussion and memorizing Scripture. The informal teaching or what I call teachable moments occur often, especially with young children who have inquisitive minds and love to ask questions. Parents should take advantage of these moments to teach, not preach, godly principles and biblical truth as they go along, *"when you walk by the way, when you lie down, and when your rise up"* (vs. 7b). Taking a walk, driving in the car, putting them to bed at night (the young ones), are great opportunities, which should be seized to teach them.

Imparting your faith to your child could and should be a pleasant experience for both of you and not something you both dread. For example, your adolescent may want to watch a television programme you don't necessarily approve of. Rather than have a big fight over it, make it an opportunity to sit with him and view the show and afterwards, discuss the morals and views expressed, weighing them against Christian values. I hasten to add that there are to be some things that a child ought not to watch or do, over which there should be no compromise. The Holy Spirit will give you new and creative ways to teach your child.

2. By Pattern. Parents impart your faith, not only in *principle* but also by *pattern.* Set a godly model for your children to follow. An anonymous quote puts it well, "Children are a great deal more apt to follow your lead than the way you point." Apostle Paul admonished young pastor Timothy, *"in all things show yourself a pattern of good works"* (Titus 2:7). Your children must see you as parents modelling godly character, such as honesty, integrity, punctuality and purity, and they must also see you reading the Word and praying.

3. By Profession. Another way to set a godly pattern is by your profession, what comes out of your mouth in their presence privately or publicly. Paul said to Timothy, *"Fight the good fight of faith, lay hold on eternal life, to which you were also called and have professed a good profession before many witnesses"* (1Tim. 6:12).

4. By Perseverance. Perseverance is key to imparting your faith to your children; do not give up in your efforts. You are to teach them diligently. The Hebrew word for diligent means "to whet," that is to sharpen or to stimulate; as in to whet their appetites through the Word's pattern of living for the true God. It is to keep their appetites stimulated for God and godliness so that when the enemy comes to entice them with worldly pleasures and sin they won't have any taste for them. What do you teach them? Teach them to be obedient to the Word of God. Teach them to pursue their God-given purpose. Teach them to live holy and pure before God. Teach them the fear of the Lord for it is the beginning of wisdom. Teach them to love the Lord their God with all their heart, soul and mind.

5. By Prayer. Persevere in **prayer**, as you do, your labour will not be in vain for it would bear fruit. Job continually covered his children, sanctified them and offered burnt offering on their behalf even though they were grown. The Scripture does not state this, but I am sure that Jochebed, Moses' mother, never ceased to pray to the God of Israel for her son after she released him into the river, and neither did Hannah when she released Samuel to God.

Pray God's will be done in their lives as it is in heaven, pray prayers of declaration, declaring the Word of God and the specific promises God has given you concerning this child. Pray for their friends, schoolmates, teachers and those who may have influence over them in any sphere of relationship. Above all, teach them to pray and declare the Word of God themselves.

CHAPTER 3
LISTEN TO YOUR CHILDREN

Let every man be quick to hear, a ready listener, slow to speak, slow to take offence and to get angry.

— *James 1:19 (AMP)*

As a child, I often heard my parents say, "Children are to be seen and not heard!" This was a common expression and belief among my parents and their peers, because that is what their parents told them. This would have contributed to the reason why many of my generation have difficulty in expressing their feelings and emotions. Even in Jesus' day, the chief priests and scribes tried to silence the children, they were offended that they were worshipping Him, crying out "Hosanna to the Son of David." Jesus by His answer sanctioned the presence of God in their lives, ***"Out of the mouth of babes and infants You have ordained praise"*** (Matthew 21:15-16). Amazingly, the children showed more spiritual insight and discernment than these learned men of the Scripture.

Your children's thoughts and feelings are important, and they deserve to be heard. Your listening conveys this message to them, "I love you enough to listen, what you have to say is important to me, even when I don't understand or may not agree with you."

Listening is an art many of us need to develop. Someone said, "God gave two ears and one mouth, so that we would practice listening twice as much as we speak."

Tips for Effective Listening

• Maintain eye contact. Looking around, glancing at the television or flipping the pages of a book or newspaper sends the message that you are not really interested or listening. This can be upsetting to anyone, especially a child. To listen effectively, there must be self-discipline and sacrifice of some of your time.

• Allow your children to express their feelings but never allow them to be rude. Try not to interrupt or formulate your answer before they are finished speaking.

• Children are more likely to share in an atmosphere that is non-threatening and not hostile. Create an atmosphere of acceptance rather than one of hostility. Give all the positive affirmation you can, nodding, smiling; these will encourage them to continue to speak.

• You may not feel like listening, but make yourself interested; this is where self-discipline comes in. It pays off in the end. You will find out lots more about the child's need and feelings if you keep tuned in. A child may want you to listen to him at a time that is truly inappropriate, such as when you are engaged in an important telephone conversation; rather than dismiss the child, simply let him know that as soon as you are through you will talk with him.

•   Learn to listen to emotions. Emotions express themselves not only in words, but also in tone of voice, facial expression, and body language. Become a student of your child to an extent that you can quickly detect changes in attitudes and behaviour and therefore know how to respond appropriately.

•   Ask questions for clarification. You may have misunderstood a point a child is trying to make; a question will help clarify and even eliminate confusion.

•   Practise empathy. You may feel that what a child has to say is insignificant. Why is he making a big deal out of this? He should grow up. But a child's feelings can be easily hurt. Therefore, it is important to show empathy, to put yourself in the child's place and try understanding his feelings.

Remember that your child is a person with feelings and emotions just like you. You pay him one of the greatest compliments by listening to him; you let him know that he and what he has to say are important to you. It also helps to promote his feelings of self-respect and self-worth. A child that is assured a ready non-judgmental listening ear in his parent is more likely to seek the advice of the parent rather than that of his peer. It is critical that this art be developed early because should your child get into any difficulty, regardless of what it is, he must feel confident that he can first come home to Mom or Dad, to a listening, non-critical, empathetic ear, before going to someone else.

CAN YOU HEAR THE CHILDREN'S CRY?

I need you Daddy.
I need you Mommy.
I need the comfort of your love,
The assurance of your protection,
The warmth of your acceptance and embrace
To secure for me a place.
The world out there is cold and dark,
I need all that you can bestow to give me a start.

Can you hear me?
I can't speak the words to say
But I hope my cries will convey
My wordless plea.

But no, they cannot hear
For there are too many voices with which to forbear.
I must wait my turn.
The sound of career calls,
The beckoning of dreams unfulfilled,
Houses and relationships to build.
I must wait my turn.

In the meantime my cries become louder,
No, not in sound or tone
But in behaviour that begs to be atoned.
They intensify like the shrill of sirens drawing near
But no one hears or even seems to care.

I still cry though, but now they are camouflaged
Like a lion in the grass waiting
To pounce on its prey.
They find expression in hate and rage
Violence and anger on the rampage.
Or, I sell my body to the highest bidder
Hoping to soothe the hurt of cries
That now loom larger.

You ask, "How come our children
Are at such a stage,
What has driven them to this place?"
I believe you hold the key to some of this disgrace.

I am older, much older now,
My children cry too, but I do not hear them either,
For I have also succumbed to the vicious
Cycle that needs to be broken.

I thought by now my own cries would have been
hushed,
So now I understand why
You couldn't hear mine.

*For beside all the other sounds that clamoured and
pushed
Your own cries were too loud
Like a radio's noisy din,
Still there in the corner screaming - still waiting;
But no one took the time to hear
Your cries within.*

— *Linda P. Jones*

CHAPTER 4:
DARE TO DISCIPLINE

*Every child should have an occasional pat
on the back as long as it is low enough and
hard enough.*

— *Bishop Fulton Sheen*

After searching several days for the strap and unable to find it, I became suspicious and asked our daughter, who was six years old at the time if she had hidden it, to which she reluctantly nodded her head. When I enquired where it was hidden, she slowly went over to the bookshelf in her room and pulled it out from under a pile of books on the bottom shelf. I had a hard time restraining myself from laughing.

The wisest man to ever live on earth, Solomon, under the inspiration of the Spirit of God said, ***"He who spares his rod hates his son, but he who loves him disciplines him promptly"*** (Proverbs 13:24). An awful indictment was pronounced against Eli, a priest in the house of God, and his sons, who were priests themselves, all because of a lack of discipline in the home. In 1Samuel 2:12 they are referred to as the "sons of Belial," which literally means, "worthless, sons of wickedness or corruption."

When Eli was very old, he made a feeble attempt to correct his sons' wicked behaviour, but they paid him no mind. If they did not listen to him as adults, it is quite likely they did not listen to him when they were children either. The Scripture goes on to say that the Lord sent a man of God to speak to Eli and one of the questions God asked him was, *"Why do you...honour your sons more than Me...?"* Eli was unwilling to punish his rebellious sons by dismissing them from the priesthood for their lewd and impious behaviour, because that meant he would lose the benefits of the wealth and plenty of the office. Consequently, the tragic end for this family was death, and an end to his posterity.

The Purpose of Biblical Discipline

The goal of biblical discipline is the development of godly character. When disciplining, a parent must be motivated by love for the child and obedience to the Word of God. There are two aspects to discipline, one is the rod and the other is reproof. The rod, which literally means "a stick for punishing" deals with punishing the external acts of disobedience and rebellion. Reproof is verbal instruction and reasoning; that is, the use of words to correct, it is not to be a tongue-lashing. Reproof deals with producing inward qualities such as honour and understanding – Proverbs 13:18 say, *"He who regards reproof will be honoured," "He who heeds reproof gets understanding"* (Proverbs 15:32).

Worldly systems today are seriously challenging a parent's right to discipline by spanking, the use of the rod. Christian parents must know that the disciplinary action of spanking is biblical. Proverbs tell us that *"Foolishness is bound in the heart of a child but the rod of correction will drive it far from him."* However, there is a clear line of demarcation between spanking and abuse. Kicking, punching, brutalising, cursing, name-calling, deprivation of food and essential needs, are clearly abusive behaviour. In an age when child abuse of every kind is practised, the parent must ensure that when he is disciplining his child, he treats "the heritage of the Lord" with love, care, respect and dignity.

Though discipline involves spanking, we must be careful to ensure that it is not always the first method we employ. It is very important then to differentiate between childish irresponsibility and wilful defiance, especially in a young child. Deliberate offensive behaviour when identified is not to be tolerated and should be dealt with appropriate disciplinary measures. It is when a parent fails to discipline his child that he makes him an "illegitimate" child. In the book of Hebrews 12:8 it states, *"If you are left without discipline, in which all have participated, then you are illegitimate children and sons."*

Moreover a child that is not disciplined becomes disrespectful, insecure and feels unloved. Not disciplining will eventually lead to shame and disgrace both to the child and parents. *"Poverty and shame shall be to him that refuses instruction"* (Proverbs 13:18a). *"But a child left to himself brings his mother to shame"* (Proverbs 29:15b). The rod and reproof together in balance with love, brings wisdom. *"The rod and reproof give wisdom"* (Proverbs 29:15). Our Heavenly Father deals with us as sons, which is why He disciplines us. We may not always like it, but it is a great comfort to know that He loves us and cares enough to correct us when we go wrong. We earthly parents under God are to emulate His example.

A Parent's Guide to Discipline

1. Discipline should begin promptly. *"He that spares his rod hates his son: but he that loves him chastens him betimes"* (Proverbs 13:24). "Betimes" means early in life, as Bible commentator John Gill puts it, "in the morning of his infancy, before vicious habits are contracted or he gets accustomed to sinning and hardened in it." The moment an infant begins to display a determined will, that is, to choose his own way, is when discipline should start. A child trained to be obedient to his parents is more likely to respect and be obedient to authority in society, and most of all the supreme authority, His Heavenly Father.

2. Be consistent and prompt in carrying out disciplinary action: do not threaten and not

follow through, if you do, after a while the child disregards the correction and the threats.

3. A child should know why he is being disciplined. Therefore it is necessary to have clearly defined limits of behaviour, and he must also understand the rules and reasons for them and the consequences of crossing those limits.

4. A beneficial way to discipline is to highlight the positive: complimenting and rewarding good behaviours can motivate a child to choose the desired conduct.

5. Be aware of your child's temperament. For some just mention of the 'S' (strap) word brings immediate contrition, but for others withdrawing of some privileges such as watching a favourite television show or playtime gets the message across. Spanking is not a cure all for misbehaviour.

6. Disciplining should be done in private. Never destroy a child's self-respect by embarrassing him in front of peers or adults.

7. Distinguish between the misbehaviour and the child, censure what the child has done wrong but not the child. Discipline is to be motivated by love and never done in anger. Unleashing harsh words will demoralize the child and destroy his self-esteem.

8. Spanks should be administered on that well-padded area of the anatomy God provided. Use a selected and neutral object like a strap; not the broom, pots or the item nearest you, not even your hand if possible. Your hand should be seen as an object of love, to hold, caress, to hug and to give a comforting touch. For a small child, a slap on the wrist is permissible, especially if he is touching something that could bring him harm.

9. Always let the Word of God be the standard on which you base your discipline. Explain to the child why their actions or attitudes are wrong and what is acceptable according to the Word.

10. Let there be a time of reassuring of your love and acceptance after the discipline is over.

CHAPTER 5
BLESS AND NOT BLAST

Pleasant words are a honeycomb, sweet to the soul, and health to the bones.

— *Proverbs 16:24*

One of the meanings of the word *"blast"* according to Webster's Dictionary is "to curse, to shrivel or wither; arrest in growth; blight, ruin or destroy." What a contrast to the meaning of *"bless"* which is "to praise, to cause to prosper, to empower, to excel." Lloyd Ogilivie in his book "Lord of the Impossible," stated that "to be a blessed person is to know, feel and relish God's affirmation, assurance, acceptance and approval. It is the experience of being chosen and cherished, valued and enjoyed." He went on to explain that if the sense of blessing, which is, approval, praise and affirmation has been denied us by our parents and significant persons, while we were growing up, we find difficulty in allowing God to bless us. It can therefore be seen that having a sense of being blessed is paramount not only to our child's social and emotional development, but also to his spiritual well-being and healthy relationship with his Heavenly Father.

Words Have Power

Proverbs 18:21 states, *"Death and life are in the power of the tongue: and those who love it will eat its fruit."* It is through the power of the tongue that we bless or blast. Another word that could be used for blast is "curse." It carries the meaning: to despise, bring into contempt, to lightly esteem, to malign, *to stab with words.* Through the power of the spoken word, parents can frame their child's world. They either bless with positive words of love and affirmation, propelling them into their God-designed destiny, or blast them with negative debilitating words which cause them to shrivel, wither and eventually come to ruin unless there is a supernatural intervention by God. Whichever the parent chooses: words of life or words of death, they are guaranteed to *eat* the results of them. It reminds one of the saying of a person, "having to eat his words."

Learning from the Patriarchs

The Old Testament patriarchs practised pronouncing blessings on their children. They spoke words of high value and pictured a future for their children. Isaac blessed Jacob with a beautiful picture of his future, he said, *"...May God give you of the dew of heaven, of the fatness of the earth, and plenty of grain and wine. Let peoples serve you, and nations bow down to you..."* (Genesis 27:28-29). A generation later, Jacob blessed his sons. One in particular is Judah. Of Judah he said, *"Judah you are he whom your brothers shall praise; your hand shall be on the neck of your enemies; your father's children shall bow down before you..."* (Genesis 49:8-9): a blessing that has surely materialized, for out of the line of Judah came our Saviour and King, Jesus Christ the conquering Lion of the Tribe of Judah. Parents, stop and consider the power of your words on the future destiny of your child.

Consider Esau, Isaac's firstborn, the one who had the special right to the first-born blessing, but who in a moment of weakness sold it to his younger brother Jacob for a bowl of stew to gratify a temporary hunger pang. The time came when he requested his blessing, and only then recognized the folly of his ways and the grave consequence of his actions. In anguish, he cried out to his father, *"Have you only one blessing, my father? Bless me, even me also, O my father! And Esau lifted up his voice and wept"* (Genesis 27:38). What pain resonates in those words as he pleaded for a blessing; a blessing he had previously treated with contempt. He did receive a blessing, but not the one he was entitled to, because the blessing once spoken cannot be revoked. The result was that Esau became angry and hateful towards Jacob (Genesis 27:42).

In an attempt to win back his father's favor, he married the daughter of Ishmael, his father's half-brother, when he realized that the daughters of Canaan did not please his father (Gen. 28:8-9). We meet people like Esau everyday, at work, in church, or in the marketplace, who are silently crying out by their actions and words for the blessing that was never bestowed on them.

The Heavenly Father set the example for us as parents in Genesis, the book of beginnings. After creating man in his own image, *"God blessed them and God said to them, be fruitful and multiply; fill the earth and subdue it..."* (Gen. 1:28). The blessing God spoke gave man direction into his purpose and destiny. Blessing children was also part of Jesus' ministry while on earth. When the disciples wanted to stop the children from "disturbing" Jesus, He was greatly displeased, but instead took them up in His arms and laid His hands on them and blessed them. He exemplified with this act that children's genuine need is to be blessed and more so, they were at the heart of the kingdom of God (Mark 10:14,15).

In almost every instance when a blessing was bestowed, touching or embracing accompanied the words. Jesus took the children in His arms and put His hands on them. Jacob was hugged and kissed by his father Isaac as he received the blessing. Much later on he, Jacob, stretched out his hands and laid them on the heads of his grandsons, Ephraim and Manasseh as he blessed them.

Studies have shown that there are therapeutic benefits in meaningful touching. In the Caribbean, we were not accustomed to having our parents hug and kiss us and touch us in meaningful ways. Consequently, we shun doing the same to our children and as a result, we deny them the physical and emotional benefits, and also neglect an important biblical principle. Children who have not been properly touched and correctly affirmed, eventually seek for it in all the wrong places and from the wrong people.

Practising the Blessing

In many orthodox Jewish homes, the family blessing is still practised today. Each week there is a ceremony with lit candles etc., where the father pronounces a blessing on each of his children. What a difference it would make to our children and their generation, if Christian parents who know the Messiah and the blessings which He has bought for them, through His death on the cross and His resurrection, practise blessing their children on a regular basis. What a difference it would make as we communicate words of high value, love, respect, affirmation and acceptance; words that give a sense of identity and prophesy, a dynamic godly future for them.

Our children face a barrage of blasting from the world, many times beginning right outside their doorsteps from peers and adults alike. It is vitally important that as parents we create an atmosphere of blessing in the home. It has been said, cursed people do not survive, and this is so true. Our children are called to excel and be a blessing to their generation and to the nations.

The Blessing:

Don't let your children leave home without it.

> *"The Lord bless you and keep you;*
> *The Lord make His face shine upon you,*
> *and be gracious to you; The Lord lift up His*
> *countenance upon you, and give you peace"*
> *(Numbers 6:24-26).*

Children Learn What They Live

> *If a child lives with criticism,*
> *He learns to condemn.*
> *If a child lives with hostility*
> *He learns to fight.*
> *If he lives with ridicule*
> *He learns to be shy.*
> *If a child lives with shame,*
> *He learns to feel guilty.*
> *If a child lives with tolerance,*
> *He learns to be patient.*
> *If a child lives with encouragement,*
> *He learns confidence*
> *If a child lives with praise,*
> *He learns to appreciate.*

> *Courtesy PAREDOS*

CHAPTER 6
BUILDING SELF-ESTEEM

Parents need to fill a child's bucket of self-esteem so high that the rest of the world can't poke enough holes to drain it dry.

— *Alvin Price*

My personal struggle with low self-esteem for many years, has equipped me in an unexpected way to write about this subject. I am still learning new ways of thinking, and unlearning negative thought patterns and behaviour. I confess that I haven't done it all right where my daughter is concerned, but we are both growing and learning together. As my Heavenly Father heals and teaches me, I impart to her.

I hesitated to write on this topic of self-esteem, because I believe that if the principles from the previous chapters in this book were put into the practice, the natural outcome would be a child with a healthy self-esteem. Nevertheless it would not harm to reiterate some of these principles and expand on others.

What is Self-Esteem?

Self-esteem very simply is the way one feels about oneself. It is a combination of feelings and perception one has of oneself. It influences how one sees the world, how one interacts with others, and how one deals with everyday situations. One's self-esteem becomes like a set of lenses through which reality is perceived. In essence, one's perception becomes one's reality. A child with good self-esteem grows up feeling significant; he likes himself, can relate well with others and has the ability to stand up in difficult situations. In contrast, one with low self-esteem grows up with feelings of inadequacy. He fears rejection, yet he looks to others to validate him. He struggles to be accepted by others, but does not accept himself. He lives in a state of ambivalence.

Some Strategies for Building Esteem

Building a child's self-esteem starts with the parent. It starts from the womb, the place of conception. The parent, especially the mother, must examine her feelings regarding the pregnancy. There might have been the feeling that it was not a "convenient" time to have a child or that a new baby would cause severe financial stress on the family.

There might also have been the feelings of guilt, shame and condemnation if the child was conceived outside of wedlock, or the mother might secretly have wished she were never pregnant. Perhaps also, the father on becoming aware of his new responsibility, became scared and abandoned the mother, causing her to become angry with him and the child for the weight of responsibility thrust on her. Situations like these have negative impact on the mother and her unborn child.

Parents need to be aware that words and emotions are transmitted into the womb and received by the foetus. The workings of the Spirit of God are also transmitted and received. The unborn child is an active, responsive person. The story in Luke 1:15 is a good example of this, it states that John the Baptist was filled with the Holy Spirit from his mother Elizabeth's womb. Later on when Mary the mother of Jesus greeted Elizabeth, baby John responded by leaping in her womb for joy (Luke 1:41-44). It is therefore very critical for parents to realize that they can begin to communicate words, thoughts and emotions of acceptance and love to their child from as early as conception.

As that child begins to grow and develop, a great deal of his self-image is formed from the perceptions he has about the way his parents "see" him. What a parent communicates in words and unconscious attitudes convey worlds of information about what that parent thinks the child is, and these perceptions form the core of the child's self-concept and personality. For example, a child may do something foolish, but the parent's response in correcting may convey to him that he is foolish; or the child may behave in ways that disappoint the parent, but rather than deal with the behaviour, the parent conveys the message that the child is a disappointment. It is very easy for this to happen.

Often we as parents have high expectations for our children; we almost want them to be perfect, when we ourselves are not, and in our quest for this, we become frustrated and angry with them for not meeting our expectations. My mother always said, "Actions speak louder than words," but I would like to add, "Attitudes and actions speak louder than words." It is not only the traumatic experiences that influence a child's self-image, but also the everyday experiences. The general atmosphere of the home influences his self-image; and a child senses and internalizes these feelings, actions and attitudes toward him.

However, we must never underestimate the power of words. As we saw earlier, we can either bless or blast our children with our words. It is not uncommon to hear parents calling their child such names as, "idiot," "stupid," and "wicked," or for them to make comparisons between them and another sibling or their friend's child, saying, "Why can't you be like so and so?" These and similar statements are devastating to a child's personhood; they say to him that he does not have worth in your eyes and you do not love and accept him for who he is.

It is not enough to only love your child, but it is important to convey respect. A child is to be respected for the gift he is from God, remember Psalm 127:3-5. When you value someone you will respect him. Genuine love and respect from a parent are the primary ingredients in establishing a child's esteem and helping him to believe in himself.

However, parents and the quality of home life are not the only factors that influence a child's life. A child receives input from friends, peers, teachers, other members of the family and society as a whole. These influences either reinforce or are in opposition to what a child has been taught in the home, and are not easy to control. It is therefore the parent's responsibility to strengthen a child's self-esteem so when he faces rejection, ridicule, and cruel name-calling from these external influences, he will not be crushed, but would be resilient and grow and develop into a healthy person.

There are other practical ways a parent can help contribute to the building of the child's self-esteem such as exposing the child to new and interesting learning experiences. It helps to expand his intelligence and increase his confidence and competence. Help your child to discover something he can do well and excel in. Train him up in the way he is inclined, or bent, for when he is old he will not depart from it (Proverbs 22:6). In this culture, there is pressure to excel in academics, but that may not be your child's greatest strength or interest, maybe it is an artistic ability, a love for a particular sport or music. Whatever it is, you will do him a great service by being his number one supporter and coach, encouraging him to excel in that particular area. This will give him a tremendous sense of well-being, confidence and accomplishment, and he will be a happier child.

Biblical Examples for Instilling Self-Esteem

Jacob's self-concept was prophesied through his name, which means "trickster, deceiver." Every time his name was called, it reinforced to him who he was, and as the Scripture bears witness, he lived out his name in character. However, God came on the scene and confronted that negative judgment on his life and affirmed him for who he truly was meant to be. He renamed him Israel, saying, *"Your name is Jacob; your name shall not be called Jacob anymore, but Israel shall be your name"* (Genesis 35:10). Israel means Prince with God. Out of the loins of Jacob came the twelve tribes of Israel. This declaration cancelled the curse spoken over his life through his name.

Gideon had a real self-esteem problem. When called by God to be a deliverer to the children of Israel, he responded in terms of how he saw himself, *"O Lord, how can I save Israel? Indeed my clan is the weakest in Manasseh, and I am, the least in my father's house"* (Judges 6:15). God knew all this before Gideon informed Him, yet that did not stop Him from calling him, "You mighty man of valour!" Gideon was used by God as a powerful instrument in liberating the Israelites from their oppressors.

The Corinthian church was experiencing all kinds of problems, including doctrinal, moral, and social issues. The Apostle Paul, the "parent" of this body of believers dealt sternly with them in his letter, but at the same time he openly expressed his love and confidence in them. He communicated respect and value to them, *"I have great confidence in you; I take great pride in you"* (2Corinthians 7:4). *"I am glad I can have complete confidence in you"* (vs. 16).

Jeremiah was the son of a priest. One would think that coming from a priestly family, Jeremiah would be very secure and he would respond readily to the call of God, but not so. As a young man, Jeremiah had internal conflict; he was afraid and timid, and felt incapable of performing the task to which God had called him (Jeremiah 1). But God just kept on affirming him and confirming who he was, and what he was called to do. Eventually, prophet Jeremiah's self-esteem was renewed; he learned to accept God's love for him, to accept himself and move on to effectively fulfil the call of God on his life.

Name your children with a prophetic purpose in mind. Declare to them that they are great through Jesus Christ, they are winners, they are children of excellence like Daniel, and they are here for God's purpose like Jeremiah. Declare to them that they are God's special treasure, mighty men and women of valour, and that they have come into the kingdom for such a time as this to impact nations. They will believe it and live it.

There are no shortcuts to building self-esteem nor is it acquired by accident. It takes concerted effort, time, perseverance, patience, praise and prayers. The results and benefits however are long term, long lasting and invaluable in the life of the child and his world. However, parents who suffer from poor self-esteem cannot give something that they do not have. This is where the healing of Father God through the power of His Word comes to bring transformation to lives. One's true identity and self-esteem are only established when we see and accept ourselves as God does.

CHAPTER 7
FOR FATHERS ONLY

The results of faithful fatherhood far outweigh any career climb, any economic windfall, or any position of power and fame that can be imagined.

— *Howard Hendricks*

The Old Testament culture was patriarchal; the father was the main authority figure in the family. At that time, his primary responsibility was religious. The father was the priest of the family and was to train his children in godly living. He was also to communicate and perpetuate a living faith in Jehovah God. Not only was he to impart a living faith to his children, but also to his entire household, the servants and attendants included. He was also responsible for the care and discipline of his family (Deuteronomy 8:5).

Abraham was such a man, he is known as the father of the Jewish nation, however, when we first met him, his spiritual roots were embedded in the paganism of his homeland, Ur of the Chaldees (Gen. 11:31). But Abraham had developed a new spiritual legacy and friendship with God to such an extent that when God was about to destroy Sodom and Gomorrah, He first confided in His trusted friend Abraham. God said of him, *"For I know him, that he will command his children and his household after him, and they shall keep the way of the Lord, to do justice and judgment ..."* (Genesis 18:19 KJV). Abraham feared or reverenced God and demonstrated this by his obedience and faithfulness to Yahweh. He kept His way and took responsibility for the spiritual welfare of his household. For this, Abraham inherited the promise of those who fear God (Psalm 25:14); the Lord shared His secrets with him. That's something to think about.

Fathers Where Art Thou?

Today's western society on the other hand, is predominantly matriarchal. The mother plays the dominant role in the home, and in many cases she is single. The presence of and contribution from the father are virtually non-existent. Some men only sire children but don't have the desire, ability or skill to nurture them. The fact is that many of these men were themselves either abandoned by their own fathers or inadequately fathered. They probably remember their fathers as being cold, distant and uncommunicative or impatient, angry and abusive, either to them or their mothers. Some came from homes where the father was lazy and unproductive, or he was an alcoholic or a workaholic, and was never at home to be involved in their lives. The mother had to perform both her role and that of the father.

Many others came from homes where the father was a rigid disciplinarian and ruled the home like an army training camp. Whatever historic background men have come from, the Scriptures provide them with many stories of the successes and failures in fatherhood, from which they can learn. However, before fathers who have come from dysfunctional homes can become effective in parenting, they must be healed from their pain and the impaired image that they have of their Heavenly Father. As one writer said, "Children do **who you are**, not what you say." How is your relationship with your Father?

You may say that since you were not fathered in a positive way, you do not know how to be a father to your children. Abraham came from a pagan background; he had no real understanding of the true God. Yet when God called him he obeyed, and set new spiritual roots for his family that were after the ways of the Lord. There is something about a call from God that empowers you to fulfil its requirements. Dads, if you have been granted the privilege of fatherhood, and have obeyed Christ's call to follow Him, then the Holy Spirit will empower you to be successful fathers.

Understanding the Importance of Your Fathering Role

Fathers need to know how critical their roles are in the development of the lives of their children. Most importantly, a child's concept of God as Father is affected by the way in which he perceives his earthly father. He unconsciously transfers to God the imperfections and weaknesses of his father. Unfortunately, we have it in the reverse, for it is from God's fathering we come to an understanding of what an earthly father should be. Christian fathers have an awesome responsibility to reflect the image of God in their relationship with their children. I emphasize "Christian" because, until Christ, who is the express image of the Father, is allowed to make His abode in the life of an individual, he cannot reflect the image of Father God.

Just as our Heavenly Father gives us our true identity as children of God, we get to know whom we are when we come into an intimate relationship with Him. Similarly, the father, more than the mother, has a significant role to play in shaping his son's identity as a male and that of his daughter as a female. Girls who do not have loving affirming relationships with their daddies, frequently look for daddy's love in the first man who shows any "interest" in her. As she gets older, she has sexual relations, not because she necessarily wants to, but because she is looking for that special love she missed from her father. It is said that girls play at sex for love while boys play at love for sex.

Boys on the other hand, have problems defining their masculinity. If a male child has difficulty in his relationship with his father, and if daddy is cold, weak, aloof or non-affirming, then this child may become involved in a homosexual relationship. He was not necessarily looking for such relationship; he was really looking for daddy, for closeness, security and protection and for the affirmation he never got. It is the quest for this emotional validation that leads many young men into unnatural sexual involvement with other men.

Lessons on Fathering from the Scripture

A Father Prays for His Child

The Apostle Paul took on the role of spiritual father of young Timothy. In his letters to Timothy, he lovingly addressed him as his dearly beloved son or his own son. The Apostle prayed fervently for this young pastor who was fulfilling the call of God upon his life, *"As without ceasing I remember you in my prayers night and day"* (2Timothy 1: 3). I am sure this was a source of great encouragement to Timothy, to know that Paul, his spiritual father, was praying for him. This is one very important way a father can bless his child, by praying for him and letting the child know that he is. Pray that God's will for that child's life will come into existence on earth as God ordained it in heaven.

A Father Shares Strategic Plans

King David was not always a model of fatherhood. He made many mistakes. He failed to keep his sexual desires under restraint; he committed adultery with Bathsheba then orchestrated her husband Uriah's death. His sons were rebellious and out of control. Actually, his whole family's life fell apart after he sinned.

In spite of this, David at the end of his life did some positive things in relation to his son Solomon who would succeed him after his death.

The responsibility for building the house of the Lord had fallen upon Solomon, and David was wise enough to encourage him in this venture and so provided the necessary building materials and other resources that were needed to accomplish the work.

David knew by the Spirit of God the plans for the building of the temple (1Chronicles 28:11-12). Then he sat down with Solomon and shared with him the details of the plans God had given him. Fathers, your children are destined to be the temples of the Holy Spirit, the temples of God (see 1Corinthians 3:16,17). If you are men of prayer and seek God's face, He will give you specific plans concerning your child's purpose and destiny that you are to share with him at the right time. As you share the good plans God has for him, you help equip and motivate him to live his life in such a way that God is pleased to inhabit him.

A Father Provides for His Child

Not only did David give Solomon the plans for the temple, he provided the appropriate workforce, the people, for getting the job done, "*...the division of the priests and the Levites, for all the work of the service of the house of the Lord*" (1Chronicles 28:13a). David knew this was not something that Solomon could accomplish on his own. A good father realizes that different types of people will impact the life of his child and he makes sure as far as possible his child is surrounded by them. *Priests and Levites*, these represent godly people who will contribute to the positive spiritual development of his child and help in the fulfilment of the purposes of God.

Then there were people skilled in workmanship for every kind of service that was needed, vs. 21 *"and every willing craftsman will be with you for all manner of workmanship, for every kind of service."* These are those who possess technical, academicals and all other types of skills that would add to a well-rounded individual.

He also provided the articles to be used in the building of the temple. *"He gave gold by weight for things of gold, for all articles used in every kind of service"* (1Chronicles 28:14-18). All the different types of materials Solomon needed for the construction of the house of the Lord were provided. These are the material resources a father needs to provide for his child; food, shelter, clothing and other material needs for a growing child.

David also provided reassurance of the promise of God. He gave moral support and encouragement to Solomon that God will be with him, and in vs.20 he said, *"Be strong and of good courage, and do it; do not fear nor be dismayed, for the Lord God - my God - will be with you, He will not leave you or forsake you until you have finished all your work for the service of the house of the Lord."* David knew first hand of God's faithfulness throughout his life, and that God was his God. He had a personal relationship with Him and could confidently declare to Solomon that this same God would never leave him nor forsake him while he accomplished the call of God on his life.

Dads, you can do the same for your children. They desperately need to know and believe in a God who is all-powerful and faithful. It is not just food and shelter that a father should provide, but spiritual and emotional support and affirmation, to encourage faith in a faithful God. These are some of the things that contribute to the development of a balanced child, things that minister to his spirit, soul and body.

A Father Pronounces Blessings on His Children

In a previous chapter, **Bless and not Blast**, the importance of the blessing and how the patriarchs of old always blessed their children before they died, was mentioned. Moses released a final blessing upon the children of Israel before he departed from them. In a sense, he was a father to the Israelites; he cared for, nurtured, directed and provided for them under God, from Egypt and during their journey through the wilderness. Exodus 33 is a beautiful chapter of the pronouncement of these blessings.

A Father Prophesies to His Children

Jacob, at the end of his life, called his sons together and told them what would happen to them in their lives

(Genesis 49). Everything he prophesied concerning his sons came to pass just as he said. Dads, prophesying to your child will encourage, edify and bring comfort to him; it will give him a picture of a future to which he can aspire.

A Father Plays with His Children

Playing is as spiritual as praying or prophesying to your child. In the midst of the training and disciplining, a father needs to have times of fun and relaxation with his children. Too often he is out busy working and providing for the family and neglects this all-important activity. Playing is a vital part of raising healthy balanced children.

A Father does not Provoke His Children

"Fathers, do not provoke your children to wrath but rather bring them up in the training and admonition of the Lord" (Ephesians 6:4). Colossians 3:21 is a similar command. In this verse, God cautions fathers not to anger their children with severe and cruel commands, not to embarrass them with public scoldings, outbursts of rage, and demeaning language. These will only make them irritated, resentful, angry and discouraged.

On the positive side, they are to "bring them up"; the word is to *nourish* them in the discipline and instruction of the Lord. Instead of nagging, harsh words or unnecessary punishment, which only engender hatred and resentment, fathers are to spend time nurturing their children in the things of God; this involves discipline and correction. They are to teach by example. It is said that if a man does not teach his children truth, others will teach them error. Take them to church, not send them. Pray for them and with them. Let God commend you as He did Abraham in Genesis 18:19, and say, *"for I know him that he will command his children and his household after him, and they shall keep the way of the Lord."*

The Example of the Father God

All fathering and all parenting should emulate the parenting of The Heavenly Father. As a Father, He sets the pattern for His children: by showing unconditional love (1Corinthians 13). God loves us regardless, and our children must know we love them even when they do not live up to our expectations.

- Father God knows every need and accepts responsibility to provide for His family (Matthew 5:43-48; Philippians 4:19).

- God is accessible; He extends to His children ready access to His presence (Hebrews 4:16).

- He gives gifts to His children (Matthew 7:11).

- He disciplines them (Hebrews 12:7-11). The Bible states that a man who does not discipline his child, hates him (Proverbs 13:24), but chastening validates him as a son (Proverbs 3:11,12).

- God assures us of a listening ear at all times. Jesus said the Father always hears Him (John 11:42).

- The Father publicly affirmed Jesus, saying, *"This is My beloved Son in whom I am well pleased"* (Matthew 3:17). Affirm your child in the presence of his peers, and even those who reject him and watch the effect on your child's confidence and self-esteem.

God places a high premium on fatherhood; He is called Father of those who have come into a family relationship with Him through Jesus Christ. He is the Ultimate Father, The Perfect Father; whatever a man wants to learn about fathering is exemplified in Him and is found in Him.

Dads, when you do the things that help to build and not destroy your child's destiny, you affect not only him but also generations to come, and the Word of God calls you a "good man." *"A good man leaves an inheritance to his children's children"* (Proverbs 13:22).

A Father's Prayer

Lord, I need your special care,
Like your earthly father, Joseph
I want to do God's will, even if I may not
always understand. Make me gentle and
selfless in the care of my family and
children;
Help me guide them in the toils and
troubles,
The happiness and wonders of this life.

Like my Father in heaven,
Make me strong in love and forgiveness
for those You entrust to my care.

No one can do these things rightly, Lord,
Without Your constant help and boundless
mercy.
Be with me always,
And may I come to You in heaven,
And all my family with me.

Amen.

—From Passionist Publications

CHAPTER 8
HELP! I AM A SINGLE PARENT

I will comfort you as a mother comforts her child.

— *Isaiah 66:13 NCV*

Single parenthood is a growing reality in today's society. With the rapid disintegration of both Christian and non-Christian marriages, more than half of our children are reared by a single parent; and in the majority of cases, that parent is the mother. However, in spite of all this, a single parent who wants to live by godly principles is aware of the responsibility to bring up the child in the fear and admonition of the Lord.

The task is enormous and at times burdensome; this parent has twice as much responsibility, twice as much demand on time, energy and resources, and half the financial and emotional support. A mother will often panic. "How am I to raise and teach these children all they need to know?" "Do I have what it takes to cope with all the demands of, and responsibility to my children, and at the same time be able to keep my life from going over the edge?" In instances where the family is separated by divorce, the mother often struggles with guilt, a sense of failure, loneliness, anger and low self-esteem. She has her own emotional struggles and at the same time must try to bring life into balance for herself and her children.

I often wonder if we who live in families where both mother and father are present, are aware of or sensitive to the pressures and struggles that single parents face on a daily basis. I think we take it for granted that they are doing well, and so we never stop to inquire or offer help in any way. I was awakened to the reality of a single mother's persistent pain as she commented, with the sound of regret in her voice. She said that she would never advise any one to have a child before getting married. She did not regret having a son, but having to cope alone without a married partner was overwhelming and frustrating. She said that at times of decision-making she would often wonder, "Am I doing the right thing?" "There is no one to bounce things off." At other times she would yell at the child because of frustration and anger. What must a parent do? Where can she go for help when she feels as though her sanity is being threatened?

Time Out for the Single Parent

There are some things a single mother can and must do for herself, especially after a divorce or separation. One very important thing is to re-establish her identity in Christ, if this is not already the case. She should also spend time with Him in prayer, worship and the Word, and open up her life to His forgiveness, healing and restoration. Regardless of the circumstances under which a mother becomes a single parent, she must have her identity soundly established in Christ, because it is in Him she lives and moves and has her being (Acts 17:28).

Another thing a single mother can do is to build a bridge of support through relationships with other single parents especially those within the church community. This allows sharing, encouraging and praying for one another. Such times can help one to maintain a proper perspective on the highs and lows of parenting. It is of great comfort when you know that you are not alone in what you are experiencing. It once was said that it takes a village to raise a child, maybe we need to get back to that practice, where the neighbourhood aunties and uncles looked out for each other and their children.

To you single mothers, your children deserve attention, but so do you. Take time for yourself. Your extended family, a trusted neighbour or friend can look after the children for a couple of hours while you go shopping. Treat yourself to a manicure or go to a show with friends sometimes. It is important to not neglect your social life; but have some time out for yourself.

The Single Parent and Her Child

Having to live without a father does not exempt a child from discipline. That child is to be raised in every aspect, as God desires. Some mothers tend to overcompensate for the absence of the father by relaxing the family rules and not creating boundaries. This will not help, but will hurt the relationship with your child. More than ever, boundaries are needed, which will be tested, but which are necessary for emotional development. A child should never be confused about what is acceptable or isn't.

A child should also be made to help with the chores around the house so that the mother does not become a slave. Teach responsibility and the child will become responsible. The goal is to maintain balance. There are times when things will not work out and this requires flexibility. Encourage yourself that you are doing the best you can under God.

Mothers, your son must not be expected to take the place of the absent father. He is not the "little man" of the house. He is a child and is to be treated as such. Do not rob him of his childhood. Do not rob him of his respect for his father either. Some mothers when in a fit of anger may make hateful, ridiculing remarks against the father. I grew up hearing adults make slurs like, "Your father is no good," "He is worthless," "He doesn't care about his children," and you can add to that list. If you feel anger and disappointment toward the father, do not display or verbalize it in the presence of the child.

Your child is not to be used as a pawn against his father by withholding visiting rights because you are angry. This is not fair to the child, his best interest must be considered. Of course, if you have proof that the father is harming the child in any way, by all means suspend communication and have the matter investigated.

In spite of your personal feelings toward your child's father, protect your child from those feelings of hatred and resentment. Help him to fulfil God's command, to honour his father and you, his mother, so that his life may be long and fruitful. Remember, your goal is to raise a godly child for the kingdom of God.

Comfort for the Single Parent from God's Promises

I believe God dispenses an extra measure of grace to the single parent. He gives special encouragement through His Word to empower that parent to accomplish the task of raising godly children.

- When you have failed and repented, God will forgive you (Colossians 1:13-14; 1John 1:9). Forget the former things, He is about to do a new thing in your life (Isaiah 43:18-19).

- When you are lonely, He is your Husband (Isaiah 54:5).

- He is a Father to the fatherless (Psalm 68:5). *"Leave your fatherless children, I will preserve them alive; and let your widows trust in Me"*

(Jeremiah 49:11). God takes the place of the parent to your children and takes personal responsibility to disciple, instruct and teach your children. The Lord will guide them in the way of salvation and the end result is that they will have peace (Isaiah 54:13).

• He is your Protector, He will see that you get justice; He will save you from oppression and wrong. God is against the perverting of justice that is due the stranger, the fatherless and the widow (Deuteronomy 24:17). Remember the story of the widow and the unjust judge in Luke 18:2-7? God, who is just, promises to vindicate the cause of His elect who cry out day and night to Him.

• He is your Provider; He provides security to the solitary, by setting them in families (Psalm 37:25). From the beginning, God is a God of families. Single parenting is not His ideal, so He takes the responsibility to establish the lonely, the widow and the fatherless in families, or "houses" as that word is correctly translated. He provides for your needs and never leaves the righteous forsaken or his children destitute for bread, the necessities of life (Psalm 37:25). He promises to liberally supply to the full your every need according to His riches in glory (Philippians 4:19).

- When you feel that you cannot take it anymore, He will strengthen your inner self (Ephesians 3:16-20). God girds you with strength (Psalm 18:32).

- When unhappiness and depression threatens to overwhelm you, He will keep your heart and mind in His peace (Philippians 4:7). Christ wants your joy to be full and to remain in you (John 15: 9-11).

Single parent, you have the enabling power of the Holy Spirit residing in you. All that you need is already in you to be a success at parenting. Do what you know to be right and just, living holy before God and He will honor your efforts.

CHAPTER 9
WHERE DID WE GO WRONG?

Making the decision to have a child is momentous. It is to decide forever to have your heart go walking around outside your body.

— *Elizabeth Stone*

Jeff was brought up in what could be perceived as the perfect home. His parents dedicated him at birth to the Lord. They provided all the love, discipline, security education, and godly training that were necessary for him to be a successful adult and Christian. They taught by principle and pattern. They weren't perfect parents but they were good parents and did their best for him. At Sunday school he was an exemplary student. Yet, at sixteen, Jeff turned his back on God and all the values he was taught, and went his own way. His parents were devastated and bewildered; they were left wondering, "Where did we go wrong?" "What could we have done differently?"

Here Comes Samson

There is a similar story in the Bible, in the Book of Judges 13, of Samson, a chosen deliverer of the children of Israel. God specially chose Manoah and his wife to be Samson's parents. Samson was destined for greatness. He was from the tribe of Dan. Jacob his forefather had prophesied, *"Dan would judge his people as one of the tribes of Israel. Dan shall be a serpent by the way, a viper by the path, that bites the horse's heels so that its rider shall fall backward"* (Genesis 49:16-17). Samson had inherited a very powerful generational prophetic blessing. His very name means "like the sun, strength"; also, there is inference of meaning, "of one prepared for battle." He was filled with the power of God to battle against the power of darkness.

The people of Israel were severely oppressed by the Philistines; they were under judgment from God because of their evil and disobedience. God wanted to deliver them and so He raised up Samson as one of the deliverers. His mother was barren but she had a divine visitation from the Angel of the Lord who gave her a promise that she would conceive a son. She was also given a prophetic word concerning his future (Judges 13:3-5). He also told her how to care herself during pregnancy and also to see to it that he was trained under the laws of the Nazarite. A Nazarite is one who was set apart for God for a special purpose. Samson was set apart for the purposes of God before he was born.

Samson's parents were obviously godly people who feared God and wanted to do the right thing. They were not satisfied with the instructions they had received, and so prayed that the "Man of God" who visited them before would come again to teach them what to do for the child (Judges 13:8). What dedication they showed to God's plan! (Samson's birth is one of the four recorded in Scripture that were heralded by an angelic visitation to the parents). They must have felt very privileged to be chosen by God for such a calling and they took it seriously. When they asked the Angel of the Lord to teach them what to do, they were asking for all the help and direction necessary to train their son so that he would fulfil the call of God on his life. *Teach* comes from the Hebrew word *yarah*, which means, "to flow as water (i.e. rain), to lay or throw (especially an arrow, i.e. to shoot); to point out as if by aiming the finger, to teach, to instruct." They realized that if they were going to aim and launch Samson as an arrow to hit the target for the purposes of God, they would need divine instructions.

His parents fulfilled their responsibility. Samson matured and the prophetic words given by the Lord began to be fulfilled. Nevertheless, Samson never crucified the fleshly passions and consequently lived according to the desires of his will. The enticement of the lust of the flesh, the lust of the eyes, and the pride of life (1John 2:16) overcame him. In the beginning God "overlooked" these sinful tendencies and used them to His own advantage (Read Judges 13-16). But in the end, the Spirit of the Lord departed from him and instead of him overcoming the enemy, they took him captive. What a waste you may say! What happened to all the prayer, the godly training and godly example? Was it to no avail?

The Reality Check

The equation of love plus consistent discipline, biblical teaching and education equal godly children is not always so. This is a reality many parents face. What are parents to do? The truth is that there is only so much that parents can do for their children; the rest is between the child and God. But there is hope and encouragement as we look at how the Triune God treats us. The Father keeps loving, caring, providing, disciplining and protecting us. Jesus is at the right hand of the Father, making intercession for us. He prays for us without ceasing (Hebrews 7:25). When we turn our backs on God, he never gives up. Jesus still prays and the Holy Spirit continually draws our hearts back to the Father and back to the relationship we once had with Him. There is no place a rebellious child can go to escape God and the call on his life. David put it so poignantly in Psalm 139:7-12. *"Where can I go from Your Spirit? Or where can I flee from Your presence? If I ascend into heaven, You are there; if I make my bed in hell, behold You are there..."*

As godly parents, our responsibility is to employ our efforts, energy and prayers on behalf of our children. Teach them all that we know to be right and godly; live what we teach before them, and entrust them into the hands of their Heavenly Father. He has centuries of experience at parenting. Keep on doing what the father of the Prodigal son did. He had a calf he was fattening for the occasion of his son's return, and he kept looking out for him. One day the son "came to himself" (Luke 15:17); he remembered how much he was loved at home, how secure he was in his father's house. When he was returning, his father saw him afar off. He ran to him, hugged and kissed him and welcomed him home. One day Samson remembered to call on the Lord God, and the Lord answered.

What if you didn't do it "right" in the beginning? No parent does it right all the time. We all make mistakes; some just make more than others. But as long as you are in covenant with the true and living God, He is faithful to His promises and to His covenant with you. When you have committed your children into His hands He promised that he would keep them. His word gives us a powerful promise by the mouth of the prophet Jeremiah that a parent can claim for a child that has strayed from the path.

> *"A voice was heard in Ramah,*
> *Lamentation and bitter weeping*
> *Rachel weeping for her children,*
> *Refusing to be comforted for her children,*
> *Because they are no more."*

Thus says the Lord:

> *"Refrain your voice from weeping,*
> *And your eyes from tears;*
> *For your work shall be rewarded,*
> *Says the Lord,*

And they shall come back from the
Land of the enemy.
There is hope in your future, says the Lord,
That your children shall come back
To their own border.

Jeremiah 31:15-17

Memo From a Child to Parents

1. Don't spoil me. I know quite well that I ought not to have all I ask for. I'm only testing you.

2. Don't be afraid to be firm with me. I prefer it, it makes me feel secure.

3. Don't correct me in front of people if you can help it. I'll take much more notice if you talk quietly with me in private.

4. Don't always protect me from consequences. I need to learn the painful way sometimes.

5. Don't nag. If you do, I shall have to protect myself by appearing deaf.

6. Don't put me off when I ask questions. If you do, you will find that I stop asking and seek my information elsewhere.

7. Don't be inconsistent. That completely confuses me and makes me lose faith in you.

8. Don't ever suggest that you are perfect or infallible. It gives me too great a shock when I discover that you are neither.

9. Don't ever think that it is beneath your dignity to apologize to me. An honest apology makes me feel surprisingly warm towards you.

10. Don't forget how quickly I am growing up. It must be difficult for you to keep pace with me, but please do try.

11. Don't forget that I don't thrive without lots of love and understanding, but I don't need to tell you. Do I?

12. Please keep yourself fit and healthy, I need you.

Courtesy PAREDOS

CHAPTER 10
WHEN IT'S TIME TO LET GO

Remember your basic assignment as a parent is to work yourself out of a job.

— *Paul Lewis*

Hannah was faithful to keep her vow to the Lord all the days of Samuel's life. She had vowed that if the Lord would give her a child, breaking the stigma of her barrenness, she would give him back to the Lord. But first she weaned him, then she took him up to the tabernacle at Shiloh that he might appear before the Lord and remain there forever. Hannah did all that was loving, nurturing and necessary to prepare Samuel to be returned to the Lord for His use. It must have been a difficult time for her to finally release her son.

Facing the Inevitable

Mary and Joseph must have been a bit stunned if not stung by Jesus' response to them. They complained to Him, when he was twelve years old, about how worried they had been for not being able to find Him for three days during the Feast of the Passover. Jesus made it clear that He was in good hands because He was about His Father's business. Scripture tells us that He went home and was subject to them. They did not quite understand what Jesus meant, but Mary kept these things in her heart (Luke 2:41-52). I believe from that time on as a mother, deep within herself she suspected that completely releasing her Son was only a matter of time. He was not theirs to possess.

Letting go of a child does not come easy. Releasing a child can be a painful and heart-rending process for the parents. The tendency is to hang on. Some parents even attempt to live their lives vicariously through their children and this causes all kinds of relational problems. It is important that we prepare ourselves and our children for this experience. This will make it less traumatic for the entire family, resulting in a much easier transition.

Remember that our children are only on loan to us from God, they are His, and we are just temporary custodians of them. It is interesting to note that when a child takes his first steps, from then on he starts *walking* away from his parents. He instinctively begins to assert his independence. Parents, we are like the servants to whom the master gave the talents to invest, and from whom he came back later seeking a return on his investments. We are to invest our time, love, discipline and all the other things suggested in this book, and then release our children into the hands of the Lord and into their world to impact it.

Learning From Jesus' Example

Jesus understood the pain of separating from, and releasing His disciples. He spent three and a half years of His life with them. They laughed, they cried, ate, slept, and shared joys and pain together; they were a family. Then the time came for Him to be separated from them, He had to return to His Father. Jesus had to release them as His representatives in the earth. They now had to prove, and put into practice all He had taught them in word and by example. But before he left them however, John, the beloved disciple, recorded in his gospel the last and most powerful words Jesus spoke to them. Jesus did not just send them off, instead He spent some intimate time with them at supper sharing His heart with them.

- He taught His disciples that true greatness was found in servanthood, and He exemplified this by washing their feet (John 13:14).

- He told them not to be fearful or anxious but have faith in God (John 14:1).

- He promised them His peace (John 14:27).

- He assured them of His love for them (John 15:9).

- He told them to remember the words He spoke to them during difficult times (John 16:1-4).

- He assured them of the comfort of the Helper, the Holy Spirit (John 14:15-17; 16:5-15).

- He comforted them by reminding them that though there will be times of sorrow, they were only temporary, and that these will be turned to joy (John 16:20).

- In time of need they only have to ask (John 16:24).

- The last and most powerful thing John recorded that Jesus did was that He prayed for His disciples (John 17).

This is a beautiful picture of encouragement which parents can emulate as they release their grown children. Jesus' prayer for His disciples did not end at John 17. The apostle Paul said that Jesus continues to pray; *"He ever lives to make intercession for us"* (Romans 8:34). He is at the Father's right hand making unceasing intercession for His followers.

The Old Testament patriarch, Job, regularly prayed and sanctified his children by making burnt offerings on their behalf to the Lord (Job 1:1-5). Apostle Paul wrote Timothy, his son in the Lord, and who was now in the ministry, telling him how he prayed for him without ceasing day and night (2Timothy 1:3).

Parents, having done all you can, release that child into the loving hands of a caring Heavenly Father and bathe him in prayer daily. Then watch and see what God will do, as for this child you pray.

This Child is Yours

This child is yours to guide for precious years
To build his dreams, to calm his fears
And love him, that's all you really need to do
How can you not, when he is part of you.

You put self last, you swallow pain or hurt
His careless words or action may have wrought
You smile, encourage, love and love the more
You feel his joys you know when he's down, for
This is your son.

This boy, born of a caring man and wife
This babe, the heir to all the miracle of life
Will take your heart and use it as his own
You'll never have it back, though fully grown
He's still your son.

Mould him, knowing that one day he'll go
And show him by example all you know
Give him support with lots of hugs and praise
Use common sense with love and you will raise
A loving son.

—Anonymous

LINDA P. JONES

APPENDIX 1

Scriptural Declarations to Make Over Your Children

- All my children shall be taught of the Lord and great shall be their peace (Isaiah 54:13).

- My sons shall come from afar and my daughters shall be nursed at my side (Isaiah 60:4b).

- The Lord shall increase me more and more, me and my children (Psalm 115:14).

- My seed shall be great and my offspring as the grass of the earth (Job 5:25).

- As a just man, I walk in my integrity: my children are blessed after me (Proverbs 20:7).

- I shall dwell in prosperity, and my descendents shall inherit the earth (Psalm 25:13).

- In the fear of the Lord is strong confidence and my children shall have a place of refuge (Proverbs 14:26).

- My seed shall be mighty upon earth; the generation of the upright shall be blessed (Psalm 112:2).

- My children increase in wisdom and stature, and in favour with God and men (Luke 2:52).

- As for me and my house, we will serve the Lord (Joshua 24:15).

- My son hears the instruction of his father and does not forsake the law of his mother (Proverbs 1:8).

- Enfolded in love, my child is growing up in every way and in all things unto Him, Who is the Head, Christ, the Messiah (Ephesians 4:15).

- My child is a youth without blemish, well favoured in appearance and skilful in all wisdom, knowledge, competent to stand and serve in his/her place of service (Daniel 1:4, 17a).

- My child will distinguish himself above others because an excellent spirit is in him (Daniel 6:3).

- God blesses those who bless my child and curses those who curse him; in him all the families of the earth shall be blessed (Genesis 12:3).

- My child has been formed in the womb by God, sanctified and ordained to be a prophet to the nations (Jeremiah 1:5).

- My child's gift makes room for him, and brings him before great men (Proverbs 18:16).

- The Lord will pour out His Spirit upon all flesh; and my sons and daughters shall prophesy and shall see visions (Joel 2:28).

- My child will do what is right in the sight of the Lord and walk in His ways and not turn aside to the right or to the left (2Chronicles 34:2).

- My child shall know His God and shall be strong and do great exploits (Daniel 11:32).

- My child's friends and companions are wise and pursue knowledge and understanding (Proverbs 13:20).

- My child will be an example to believers in speech, in conduct, in love, in spirit, in faith, and purity (1Timothy 4:12).

- My child does not walk in the ways of the ungodly, nor stand in the way of sinners, nor sit in the seat of the scornful; but he delights in the law of God continually, and as a result is like a tree planted by the rivers of living water and lives a fruitful and prosperous life (Psalm 1).

- My child has purpose and destiny, for he has come into the kingdom for such a time as this (Esther 4:14).

APPENDIX 2

Some Prayers and Petitions of Bible Parents for their Children

- **Abraham for Ishmael.**
  "Oh, that Ishmael might live before you" (Genesis 17:18).

- **Isaac for his grandchildren, Ephraim and Manasseh.**
  "God, before whom my fathers Abraham and Isaac walked, the God who has fed me all my life long to this day…bless the lads; let my name be named upon them, and the name of my fathers Abraham and Isaac; and let them grow into a multitude in the midst of the earth" (Genesis 48:15-16).

- **Samson's mother for the promise child Samson.**
  "O my Lord, please let the Man of God whom you sent come to us again and teach us what we shall do for the child who will be born" (Judges 13:8).

- **Samson's father, Manoah.**
  "Now let Your words come to pass! What will be the boy's rule of life, and his work?" (Judges 13:12).

- **David for his son Solomon.**
  "And give my son Solomon a loyal heart to keep

Your commandments and Your testimonies and Your statutes, to do all these things, and to build the temple for which I made provision" (1Chronciles 29:19).

- **The Syrophenician woman for her daughter.**
  "Have mercy on me, O Lord, Son of David! My daughter is severely demon-possessed" (Matthew 15:22).

- **Father of epileptic son.**
  "Lord, have mercy on my son, for he is an epileptic and suffers severely; for he often falls into the fire and often into the water" (Matthew 17:15).

- **Mother of the sons of Zebedee.**
  "Grant that these my two sons of mine may sit, one on Your right hand and the other on the left, in Your kingdom" (Matthew 20:21).

- **Jairius, ruler of the synagogue for his daughter.**
  "My little daughter lies at the point of death. Come and lay Your hands on her, that she may be healed, and she will live" (Mark 5:23).

- **Apostle Paul for his spiritual children in the Church at Colosse.**
  "And this I pray, that your love may abound still more and more in knowledge and all discernment, that you may approve the things that are excellent, that you may be sincere and without

offence till the day of Christ, being filled with the fruits of righteousness which are by Jesus Christ, to the glory and praise of God" (Philippians 1:9-11).

- **Hannah praying for a son.**
"O Lord of hosts, if You will indeed look on the affliction of your maidservant and remember me, and not forget your maidservant, but will give your maidservant a male child, then I will give him to the Lord all the days of his life…" (1Samuel 1:11)

APPENDIX 3

Journaling

One of the special things you can do for your child is to journal your thoughts of love, counsel, your dreams and aspiration for him and such like. You can record not only thoughts and Scriptures but also memorable occasions in your child's development from birth to adulthood. You can attach pictures or some of his favourite artwork or scribbles that were meaningful to you as a parent.

I started a journal for my daughter from the time she was born; writing to her has given me an outlet to record things I want to say to her. Things she may be too young to understand or things I may not be around to tell her then. I try to journal several times a year, especially around birthdays and to celebrate first occasions in her life; like her first day at school, recording her reaction and expressing the emotions I experienced at that time.

Someone reminded to me that I only have seventeen to eighteen short years to influence my child; we parents need to make the best of it.

Journaling can be one of the most treasured and appreciated gifts you can give your child as he goes off to college, or leaves home to start his own life, or God forbid, if you die before he or she reaches full adulthood, you have left them with some of the things you would have liked them to know.

Other ideas for the journal are, meaningful quotations, clips of funny cartoons, songs and poems, you may even write some yourself. You can get as creative as you want.

Permit me to share a few personal excerpts from our daughter's journal with you; I hope she would not mind.

May 17th 1994

> *Today you are exactly one and a half years old, you look like you should be two or two and a half, for your height and body structure. Daddy and I are enamoured by you. It is not hard to love you at all; your loving joyful spirit makes it so easy. I pray daily that you never lose that spirit. Right now everything is so innocent with you, Oh, I wish we could shield you from the harshness of this life, but we can't, we'll try our best to build into you a spirit of courage, strength and resilience, and with that joyous attitude you already possess, we know it would put you in good standing to cope and be an over-comer.*

April 8th 1998

> *I trust when I have failed you and not lived up to your expectations as a person or woman or mother, that you can find it in your heart to forgive me, knowing that I love you intensely and my ultimate intentions were always for your best interest.*

Have fun journaling, bless your child and you'll be blessed as well.

Linda P. Jones

Recommended Books and Other Resources

It was Solomon who said there is nothing new under the sun, many books have been written about parenting over the years and the following is a list of books, some which I have benefited and drawn inspiration from, and others provided confirmation for the conclusions I shared in **For This Child I Prayed.**

Brand, Kent R and Williams, D. Charles. *8 Toughest Problems Parents Face and How to Handle Them.* Wheaton, Illinois: Tyndale House Publishers, Inc., 1987.

Dobson, James C. *Hide or Seek: How to Build Confidence in Your Child.* London, England: Hodder and Stoughton, 1982.

Ginott, Haim G. *Between Parent and Child.* London, England: Pan Books Ltd, 1970 (first published in1969).

McCloughry, Roy. *Men and Masculinity: From Power to Love.* London, England: Hodder and Stoughton, 1992.

McDowell, Josh. *Building Your Self-Image.* Wheaton, Illinois: Living Books, 1984.

Morgan, Patricia. *How to Raise Children of Destiny: Imparting Purpose From Generation to Generation.* Shippensburg, Pennsylvania: Destiny Image Publishers Inc, 1994.

Morgan, Patricia. *The Battle for the Seed; Spiritual Strategy to Preserve Our Children.* Tulsa, Oklahoma: Vincom Inc., 1991.

Ogilvie, Lloyd John. *Lord of the Impossible.* Nashville, Tennessee: Abingdon Press, 1984.

Smalley, Gary and Trent, John. *The Blessing.* Nashville, Tennessee: Thomas Nelson, Inc., 1986.

Swindoll, Charles. *You and Your Child*, Bible Study Guide. Fullerton, California: Insight for Living, 1973.

Van Pelt, Nancy. *Train Up A Child: A Guide to Successful Parenting.* Washington, D.C: Review and Herald Publishing Association, 1984.

You have read this book and realize that you truly need to know the Heavenly Father and that you need to experience His forgiveness for your sins and His empowerment to be the godly parent He has called you to be. If so, then pray this prayer to invite Jesus Christ, who is the only way to the Heavenly Father into your life.

"Dear Lord, I believe You are the Son of God and that Your death on the cross and resurrection from the dead have paid the price for me to be reconciled to my Heavenly Father. I receive Your forgiveness for my sins and make you Saviour and Lord of my life. Amen."

You are now a child of God. Find a good Bible believing assembly and begin to grow in Christ

"Therefore, if anyone is in Christ, he is a new creation; old things have passed away, Behold, all things have become new." 2 Corinthians 5:17

You may address your correspondence to:

Linda P. Jones

E-mail: walkingonwatertec@gmail.com

Facebook: facebook.com/pastorlindapjones

Website: walkingonwatertec.org

Other books by the Author:

Daily Declarations for Kingdom Kids - Ages 4-14yrs
Meditations that are geared to assist parents in teaching
their children the Scripture and how to pray.

What Aileth Thee - the penetrating question God asks
that can lead to your healing

Out of the Ashes - True stores of the lives of women
who have been restored out of the ashes of despair to
wholeness.

Made in the USA
Columbia, SC
12 July 2022

63351337R00059